Highway of Dreams

By
Maureen Anne Browne

Cyberwit.net
HIG 45 Kaushambi Kunj, Kalindipuram
Allahabad - 211011 (U.P.) India
http://www.cyberwit.net
Tel: +(91) 9415091004
E-mail: info@cyberwit.net

Printed at Replika Press.

Contents

SPRING FEVER

The sun slips over the equator
and day slips into its nightclothes later:

ice lids dripping, slithering into oblivion
to free up rivers for the rush of herring;

fragile awakenings: tiny radicals writhing, poking,
breaking out of their seed coats;

numberless embryos in shells and soft underbellies
pushing at the walls like small Samsons bursting their bonds:

the light brings them on – acres of full-eared corn,
cattle and sheep at ease in their fields, the air full of calls

and song – skylarks, warblers, trumpeter swans, frogs,
and the colours return to us as if they have just been born.

Day slips into its nightclothes – heaven changing,
the author of nature writing a new arrangement:

Leo replacing Orion, winter's signature, with a curlicue,
a stars' invitation to consider the heavens, and we do.

FREEDOM

Do not fear
little sparrow
to come to my garden
and nest in the well-leafed hedges,
broad and deep and berry-seeded,

with blackbirds, blackcaps,
chaffinches and robins.
Perch on a trellis full of clematis;
peck at peanuts, suet or breadcrumbs;
drink from a dish of water.

The garden bristling
with birds chittering, flitting
from rhododendron to spiraea,
from the lawn shorn for summer
to stone-topped walls to lonicera.

Your song will not be hindered,
no tyrants take up arms against you;
the sun will bathe you,
rain soften winter's sharpness –
spring unfolding and you a part of it.

SNOW LEOPARD

Not myth or ghost
as some suppose,
but a shy feline
who lines her natal home
with her own shed fur.
She hunts alone.

Dawn is her time,
the Himalayas what she knows.
Before the sun has bared
the mountains she's softly
padding along the ledges:
her grey and black coat,
blazing white underbelly,
merging with rocks
and snow; surefooted
on craggy surfaces, she leaps
the canyons to where she knows
the ibex and argali feed
among the poppies and sedges,
where the stream runs
through the ravine.

The scent is human,
the rocks course different,
the river bitter.

MAGPIE

The day dimmed
by a sky with nothing
but emptiness to give.

I am sitting at my desk,
pressing my mind
for a sliver of thought,
to make something of,

my eyes wander outside
to a magpie walking
the flat-topped hedge
of golden leylandii.

It is said,
a lone magpie is a bad omen,
yet here he is
brightening the moment

in a black and white suit,
sleek-tailed jacket,
shimmering hues
of green and blue.

He fled,
leaving the garden dull,
barely a breath,

the Albertine rose
a sprawl of brown bones,
the fuchsia petals, drab red,
like miniature burst balloons,
woody stemmed.

Nevertheless,
the magpie,
this thieving bird,
bringer of sorrow,
disliked,
brought light –

I pick up my pen and write.

LAMMERGEIER

Red-ringed eyes watching
for opportunities
as you stand on your pinnacle
like an ancient oracle,
hunched in a cloak of dark,
head, chest, legs,
dressed in a dishevelled plumage
of rust-coloured feathers.

Legend says
you are a killer of lambs,
fear blinds us to the real
wonder of your wings:
an eight-foot span
of curve and fringe,
of sunlit pewter
power and beauty,
as you tour your world
of Alpine skies,
gigantic banks of white cloud,
rocks, in ridges, rising
from snow-sheeted mountains
like mediaeval cathedrals,

glide, hungry-eyed,
over wadis, ledges,
salt plains, meadows,
folding down to rest
on the dolomite's

jagged edge and watch
a snow-wolf gorge her fill;

meat gone,
moments pass each staring
the other back,
snow-wolf moves on,
you move in for the bone,
swallow it whole.

SONGBIRDS IN NEW YORK

Out of the storm you come
in mass migrations
pushing on to the Hudson.

You see sky, with cloud,
you see trees, laden with leaves.

Safe places shimmering
on the Atlantic Way
you gather momentum,

fly straight into
a myriad of glass
reflecting the geography
of the heavens:
an elevated barrier
straddling Liberty Park,
thousand-foot walls rising
from the streets of New York;

falling, with countless others,
onto the sidewalk.

The yellow breast
still bright in death,
someone tender
will lift them:
black and white warblers,

juncos and yellowthroats,
thrushes and white-throated sparrows,
broken, song stolen.

SOUNDS FAMILIAR

Raised in the green pastures
that rise to meet the purple
and gold of the Catskills,
the slow days of cattle stalling,
starting, as they make their way
to another paddock.

I meet my friend, city born
and bred, on a concrete island.

Raging round us a storm
I'd never encountered:
the emphatic din of traffic,
horns honking at every corner,
high pitched laughter,
excited chatter, the hailing
of taxis in a babble of accents.

We buy roasted nuts from a vendor,
pass stalls selling fake watches,
my friend's words a constant stream
telling me everything is awesome . . .
Shsh, I plead, shsh, listen do you hear it?
Yea, noise, he says, you'll get used to it.

The shrilling continues drawing me
to a stone planter on the pavement:
in the leaf litter of miniature maples
there's no mistaking the long antennae,
the brownish back, almost cylindrical,
limbs like little shovels – crickets in the city.

HEAVEN IN A WILD FLOWER

The wild rose of the mountains,
prairies, and wayside hedges,
comes to us in singular splendour –

no man tends it.

Interpretation of love
in a tuffet of gold cradled in dove-soft petals,
pastel pink and fragrant.

A cooler season, its graces faded,
blossom falling in pieces, yet
settling softness on stony places,

bulbs, freed from their flowery shade,
brightening into shiny red caskets packed
with calcium, manganese, potassium.

When all is done, it is not done,
it will come again,
every bit as generous –

no man tends it.

BLUE HYDRANGEA

Sun glazing the hedges,
honeysuckle and fuchsia
brightening the green bushes,
Albertine roses, and a riot
of tiny, red-tinged leaves,
adorning the plain wall,

and I am taken
with plastic containers,
some holding nothing at all:

like the paint drum,
the dirty see-through bucket,
the two milk bottles,
one smaller than the other,
yet, a sense of order,
they all stand,
like naughty children, in the corner.

Two small planters
stand with them,
a terracotta and a lavender,
full of compost,
each with its own cloche –
an empty lemonade bottle,
lid on, base cut off,
to accommodate the growing
of a leaf stolen
from a blue hydrangea.

Someone, tender-eyed,
watching over them,
raising these two siblings,
making sure the bloodline continues.

FALSE ASPHODEL

Over a hundred years ago,
when snows had slipped
from bog and fen, you rose,
clear of your grassy leaves,
a straight and sturdy stem
spawning a cluster of white stars
studded gold. Legend has it
you lit the way for Persephone.

Still, you flourish
on coastlines and stream-sides
from California to Alaska,
from Australia to Africa.
At summer's close,
your white petals will be
red pods that hold your seeds;
habits, qualities, catalogued.

Your glistening stem,
an air of innocence,
death to insects, midges,
nevertheless, no threat
to bees and butterflies.
Such deft design in the common
things around, can still surprise.

SOUTH WESTERLY

All the birds have taken
to the inner rooms of Nature.

Errant branches – ivy, briars,
spurs of golden leylandii,
shaking in their hedges,
the rose-stems in their trellis.

For you do not come gentle,
but breathing thunder
from your lusty lungs battering

the black dented planter
down the lawn
until it hits the garage wall,
the brown fronds until,
too weak to hold on,
they fall from the parent palm,
lie unwanted on the path,

tormenting
the head of the rhododendron,
not sheltered,
with endless blows
until its stunning display,
of glossy leaves
and bright purple blooms,
resembles a spent bouquet.

The thorns on the Albertine
no deterrent, man no solution.

Why so brutal?

Is it because you have it in for us,
or just because you can?

NO MORE SEA

The sky still speckled with stars,
and forty of us out in a fine boat: trawling
for hours strafed by force eight gales, rain, tide.
The camaraderie, the pride, hauling in
the huge catches of carp, sturgeon, roach.
The bread of the sea certain
for the locals, the whole Soviet Union,

until we noticed the fish dying,
the sea harder and harder to reach.
Left with a salt waste, wind tossing up toxic dust
that's crossing borders contaminating crops, rivers,
the beloved boat lying, with a dozen others,
dilapidating to a rusted cradle –
people coming in shoals to see the spectral bones.

RIVER ROE

The river that runs from the Sperrins
to my homeland of Myroe, no longer used
for scutching, spinning, the washing of raw linen,

keeps on going, rushing headlong

meandering into pools, for trout and salmon,
named by fishermen: Strawberry, McCarrons,
Footbridge Hole, The Parabans,

turning the flat lands of the valley into pasture,
the vast tracts of seeded soil into acres of wheat,
barley, potatoes, the forest of oak and birch into
a haven for foxes, squirrels, badgers, birds.

This workaday river spectacular as she pushes
through the gorges, folk catch their breath
at her frothy white waters tumbling over the boulders.

The Mussenden Temple and the bulk of Benevenagh
overseeing us. We felt unshakeable – at ease in Zion.

A storm gathering pace and we are not prepared
for the water unleashed: the river swollen,
the earthen banks do not hold – the river turns

against her own creation: crops are drowning, we are failing
to save the animals, our own home from invasion.

CHAND BAORI

The Rajasthan desert
swallowing every drop of rain
that fell on it,
and no well of Sychar.

Man began to dig deep,
deeper still, until he reached
the cool water,
built back,
a 13-storey masterpiece
the world would wonder at:

huge brick diamonds,
step-edged,
interconnecting stone paths,
a temple at one end,
carved windows,
sculptured figures,
stacked pavilions,
for any pilgrim;

women came in vivid saris –
red, green, orange,
softly treading,
resting, like exotic birds
on ledges,
      descending step
           after step
              after step,
                 fetching water
for themselves.

QUESTIONING

A shadowy presence
flung out across the promontory,
tethered to the Atlantic,
the nunnery safeguards its silences
with piles of jagged rock.

She picks her steps
along the convent walk,
slippery where the sea spews
on it daily, dangerous beauty
pulling her till the path stops,
she's standing,
on a small apron stage
over the water, and clenching
a wet bent rail,
brutal being written
in sonorous syllables:
crosswinds howling, whipping the sea,
frothy backed breakers
thundering down cul-de-sacs of rock
at horrendous speed,

she, drenched with sea-spit,
nevertheless transfixed,
failing to fathom the Power
that commands all this,
why, that night in the Channel,
the winds ferocious, the sea rampant,
there was no "Peace be still"

for the women and children,
their cries unheeded,
their lifeboat smashed to pieces.

She looks to the stars, for seeing
through a glass darkly is hard.

MUSEUM

A man of wealth, status, dining
at the Captain's table
on a ship that outclassed the Olympic.

Revelling in its gravitas, celebrating
its credentials, Made in Belfast,
the future iron-clad;

crossing the Atlantic,
with shipping magnates, writers,
fashion designers, on the crest of greatness

as if in Heaven's favour –
the sea at ease, the stars radiant;
before the dawn had taken hold

he was shuddering spluttering
in ice-ridden waters buffeted by corpses
children's shoes wine bottles; unconscious;

falling falling like the Bohemian porcelain
au gratin dishes plates platters crystal glasses
Chinese bowls Japanese vases

through deeper and deeper dark
past the prying eyes of orca and shark
the glint of luminescent fish

to end up prone in the silt
with unbroken crockery, cables, davits,
baskets of laundry, silver soup ladles.

The body raided: skin, muscles, ligaments,
stripped by lumpsuckers, rattails, monkfish,
eyes gouged by shrimp and crustacean.

Down to a spine: seen, but unidentified;
the piles of porcelain never lost
their telling sign – White Star Line.

ONGUARAAHRA

The voice
of Many Waters,
comes to us
in mighty torrents
thundering
from one lake to the other,
rushing headlong over the cliff,
like the pigs of the Gerasenes,
covering the face
of the horseshoe wall
in reams of white tulle,
smooth, or embossed –
infused with shades
of palest turquoise
to deepest jade,
turning the river
to crazy paving
with threads of surf,
bringing rainbows
full circle with sun and mist.

Figures, wrapped
in yellow plastic,
making their way between
walls of red ranch fencing,
through damp to drenched,
closer to the miraculous,
taking photographs, leaving
their mark on the path to beauty—

garbage.

The Iroquois would say:
Good gone crooked.

EMPIRE TANA

You went through so much
carrying your cargo of guns, explosives,
shrapnel, across the Atlantic: lost in fog
that was smothering everything
off the coast of Casablanca, and then, caught
in a collision of a thousand tons of shipping,
fit for nothing but a barricade, just another entry
in a register of losses – date, number, name.

Those hungry for the detritus of war,
thinking you could be taken
and plundered like an oriental hunter,
hauling you to shore for breakage,
the wind in uproar, the sea battering,
slashing till the tethering snapped,
you, held fast in the arms of an Irish lough,
sheltered, and resting on a bed of stars.

Amber and white feathery anemones
carpet your walls with lavish embroidery,
wind and tide shaking cocktails
to keep your vast populations alive –
millions encrusted, sculpted, resonant
with iridescence – Dead Man's fingers,
Sea Squirts and Sponges, Cuckoo
and Father Lashers, Sand Eels and Ballen Wrasse.

MAYTIME IN THE DALES

Do not go where the strident sounds
of a busy town
break in on things,
but take the rutted road of mud and stone
paved with puddles of rain
and you'll find yourself in a bountiful spring:
the fruit of the soil on every side
drenched to the root oozing juice.
Nature has you for a while
absorbed into succulent green
under a quiet sky –
you prize the peace:
the only thing you will hear
is the bleating of sheep.
You've been freed from the carbon-coated air
and your senses breathe:
with a keener eye you see fresh-furrowed fields,
the brilliant yellow rapeseed yields,
stone walls carving out the land
like some great mediaeval plan
and everything is swathed in grass
for countless lambs,
rabbits, that throw you a glance
before they are gone,
pheasants, in coppery feathers dressed,
sauntering over the lawn.
In the middle of all this,
a farmhouse made of concrete bricks,
hay-drums gathered to the gable wall.

No-one is seen, no-one is heard.
You feel there is only you in this world,
and you've got it all.

SCREABACH

You were prized
for the stability of your stone,
its pleasing tones of pink, white, buff.
Men trudged your paths
of gravel and mud,
smothered the air with dust,
as they thrashed the sandstone
from your side, to enhance our cities
with gracious buildings –
colleges, monasteries, bridges.

Wounded, but not spent,
left to chance and time.
Healed by Nature's liniments
hazel and thorn thrive,
your ledges nesting places
for sand martins, ravens, kestrels,

your rocky outcrop favourable
to primrose, bugle, geranium,
feral goats are shy, but can be glimpsed
further up the rise.

We tread your well-worn paths
for kinder reasons,
to stand awhile on higher ground,
rinse our mind, for the going down.

MOUNTAINS

These things he knows:

blizzard breath
churning snow onto snow,
white onto white to blinding light;

sheer-faced granite
clad with ice,
blue, black, green, white;

the Khumbu glacier,
he must tackle, slipping
fast, splitting;

those who couldn't
make the dream a reality
lying dead in The Rainbow Valley.

Nevertheless,

he inches up the ridges
neck veins bulging,
hauls himself
across moraines,
crevasses,
up ice-walls, seracs,
eyes fuzzing,
lashes iced jagged,

hands bitten
till he can't feel
his fingers raw, blistered,
crampons slipping,
lungs filling with water,
six, seven breaths given
for one step forward;
wind-blasted,
gasping,
staggering on the summit
to stay upright;

nothing diminishes
the clarity of ice pinnacles,
vast and beautiful,
like the pipes
of an ethereal organ
waiting for the Maestro,

breaking through
the pain of being flawed,
into pureness
so curiously wrought
he feels cleansed
by the breath of God.

TURF FIRE

It begins
with sacrificing the innocent:
the burning of orchids,
asphodels, butterwort
and sedges with fruit on them.
The mountain is ready
for a more incisive wounding.

Three strong men,
hands and faces
tanned and blackened
from constant weathering,
take up their slanes
and head uphill, thrust

the long-handled blade
into the sponginess, push
and push with their foot, cleaving
the earth, loosening, levering
until they've freed the bars
of brownish black
from their watery graveyard,

to be thrown into barrows, thrown
out again, built into stooks,
then bigger ones still
for Summer to harden them.
They offer only a curve of resistance;

each end a little bedraggled
like a jumper unravelling –

the men have not finished:
they carry their trophies home
by the trailer-load; placing, shaping
the dishevelled collections
against a wall which shelters them
until they are taken,
in the arms of women and children,
to feed the hearths and ranges
so that folk of an evening sit reminiscing
and sniff the air like a dog
for the sheer joy of it.

THE WAYS THINGS WERE

Finding things the same
in that room felt safe:
biscuit-coloured walls,
chocolate-brown doors and knobs,
the huge stout-legged table,
topped with a green chenille cloth
and surrounded by ten chairs,
the orange-red fireplace
with a stook of turf
blazing heat,
writing its signature with fine dust
on the ledges of the over-mantle,
the single-stemmed vase,
the picture of a girl
looking down, from her sepia world,

on grandmother,
in her blousy dress of navy print,
modesty vest fixed with pins,
the 'invisible' net on her bun.
Her shoulders firm set
against ageing
she dispenses wisdom,
receives other people's business,
a bundle of remnants
for her deft fingers
that continue knitting
socks in clerical grey
for her grown-up children.

Something foreign came
and stood between
the tall sash window
and the light brown settee:
a box, with a screen,
on four tapered legs.
My peak-capped uncle,
the one for all things electrical,
twirls knobs
forward, back, pause,
assaulting the air with static;
grandmother
gives up her throne,
for a small low armless chair,
to peer through snow.

LEATHER GLOVES

She keeps them hidden
in a drawer with a lid on it,
just under the mirror
that tries to keep track of her.
On either side of the stand are hooks
overburdened with dull coloured coats,
their tails touching umbrellas,
tennis racquets, sticks:
a dishevelled medley
disturbed, rarely
except for those times when she lifts the lid
and takes out the finest of black leather
from its bed of Italian silks:

fills up the soft, sensuous sheaths
with her fingers full of memories,
her palms, with her life written all over them,
eased into the broader sleeves,
ribbed with seams on the back of them,
then clicks them shut with tiny studs
as if she is stamping approval:
a testament to be treasured,
pages weathered with use for almost a century
sturdy enough to bear travelling:
she takes down her little black psalter,
and, holding it fondly
with hands that have an affinity with it,
goes on a journey that she takes often.

When she returns
there comes the uncovering:
opening the studs,
pulling and pulling at the leather fingers and thumbs
till her hands are naked:
she tidies her gloves palm to palm,
then strokes them together with her right hand
and lays them, gently,
almost reverently, where they belong.
She is prolific: the work goes on.

CRINDLE

We knew what we'd find:

Davy, piercing blue eyes, baring the gap in his teeth with a smile,
drinking his tea in the yard as he leans on the gate, or while watching
the rain from inside the barn. He'd return the mug and work on.

Hazel, sleeves rolled on sturdy arms, keeping the fire in the range
blazing with ragged bars of turf, wiping her hands on her apron, stirring
gravy, spearing potatoes and singing the anthem for Sunday.

Audrey polishing the piano, its stanchions, and candlesticks,
the radio cabinet, made by my uncle, the spindles, and ledges
of the over-mantle; straightening the antimacassars.

Laddie, the shaggy brown dog that rarely barked, ageing
gently, mooching about the kitchen; no longer able to round up sheep
he curls under the table to watch the familiar, doze a little.

Grandmother, in dark clothes, at her black treadle sewing machine,
Singer written in gold, pushing, and pushing the wrought-iron plate
with her foot as she turns a collar, shortens a sleeve, puts pleats in a skirt.

Three miles down the road a new factory begins to impose – more
money, plenty of overtime, indoors; men whose lives were simple start
to dream of things they never had, labourers leave the land, not Davy.

BRIEF ENDURANCE

School out for the summer
I arrive at grandmother's.
Tense as the Cold War
I walk across the yard
to the shuddering green door:
the dog, tired of touring
the kitchen, thundering
into it scratching, latch bolt
bars rattling turning me rigid.

Allowed his nose-width
he shoots straight into
me panting, slabbering,
jumping at me on me
round me yelping some
murderous language
his tongue hanging his tail
flailing. He lets me go –

my aunt is in control:
she slaps her thigh
and he's bounding behind
her to be shut in
with the potato boiler
and the rusting bicycles.
She throws me a bandage –
He's only being friendly.

The sun busy beckoning:
with my cousin I crawl over
straw bales knowing
they will prick like needles,
swing on the apple trees,
meddle with machinery:
the cultivator, the tractor,
the trailer, and things left
to themselves in the defunct
stable: Tilly lamps, Rizla tins,
bone-handled knives, a graip
with a missing tine, chicken wire.

My wound salved for a while,
gravitating towards my heart,
making the going back hard.

VENICE IN LOCKDOWN

You were the centre of attention:
love blossomed on the Canalasso,
thousands of people came,
like the Queen of Sheba,
to see for themselves
her beautiful features;

marble palaces,
the works of Titian, Van Dyck, Bernini,
pretty bridges with arched windows;

now, a solitary figure,
all must keep their distance —

black-lacquered gondolas,
and vaporetti, remain tethered,
motorboats and cruisers
no longer slicing the water,
churning up mud from the bottom;

the canals are bluer,
little fishes dart and flicker,
crabs sidewalk the sand,
swans wend their way along
the clear waters,
nothing to hinder their progress,

air and light freed,
how much easier she breathes.

RIO

It was compelling:
into the cupboard
of her imagination she put

ostrich feathers, silver satin,
gladiator sandals with impossible
heels and dazzling diamanté,
rubies, sapphires; crazy music:
rock, hip hop, samba;
immaculate men bronzed to perfection,
dice rolling, the Daiquiri flowing.

Tired of the safe norms:
like the discontented pony pushing
at the fences, she left
her warm bed, friends, family,
for the magic.

Her mother, eyes tired straining,
walks the streets posting
messages of love on the walls
of back-street bars and casinos:

Come home - whatever you've done.

A PLACE TO BELONG

She shouts across the raucous looms
mouthing words, cheating the giant's clattering
of ratchet wheels, beams, battens, conversing
gaily in language with no sound, compensating
for the daily round of fetid air, sacrificing lungs to cotton
as she works the floor filling the spindles
from dawn to dusk, for pay that keeps her poor.

Taking her feet from the downy dunes
she puts on clogs, clinking the cobbles as she goes
continues on in her own world of rag and bone,
living off bread and dripping, potato peelings,
meat on Sunday, maybe; scavenging
under the market table for carrot and cabbage,
no cups in the cupboard, no butter.

Folk as queer as folk can be
the way they wear their poverty: frenzied dances
of feisty wenches pulling the eyes of leering men,
curious children chasing chances ogle it all in the drinking den.
Strident voices yelling prices from many-coloured magic stalls,
the trundling carts of muffin-men, their calls – colours
splashed on the grisly grime of fog.

The mills, the streets, in which she grew straight and strong,
are gone. She never wished it different, it gave her a place to
belong.

ACCOMMODATING

On an apron of tarmac,
outside McDonalds,
an abandoned yellow carton
with its burger half-eaten,
gum chewed, spat out, splattered,
the flash of silver a cigarette packet –
Lambert & Butler hugging the gutter,
plastic bags drifting, settling
on concrete steps, roadside edges;
a student busking on the pavement,
torn jeans, luminous green trainers,
his t-shirt proclaiming, 'you only live once',
his body swaying as he strums
Crazy Little Thing Called Love,
the guitar case open for takings,
people gathering, waiting, risking the road,
friends, strangers, sitting at tables,
apartments, houses, filling up spaces,
the square forbidden
till the workmen have finished
laying the paving;
we go on with our business,
side-stepping the fences,
taking the path marked 'Pedestrians'.

Between the car park and the school limits,
in no man's land of abandoned privet,
grass and thistle, nature's radicals pushing
up through the dark, through the tangles,
to bring us the promise of blackberries.

HIGHWAY OF DREAMS

She watches from the edge of change
Mesmerised, and more than a little afraid
For today they are laying Black

And will lay it tomorrow
And the day after that
Building a highway of dreams.

Whatever they call it
She knows, she knows that it means
The death of things.

The air is already turning foul
As the tarred earth burns
And spits out stones and oil.

On and on it goes
The shuck and shovel of hot bitmac
Covering up.

Along its broad unending back
Come TV sets and burger bars, Coco-Cola, jeans:
The neon lights of a western world

That is moving in to the cherry-blossomed hill,
To the wild places of Rampion, Alfalfa, Campanula,
To the forests of Carpathian Chamois.

Smitten by the new world's patter the young
See their chance to be part of the glamour
Along their highway of dreams.

Whatever they call it she knows the common ground
Will be gone where everyone came to work the hay
And join in the singing of songs.

LOSING PARADISE

We made it happen. Hacked, clawed
till our backs were sore. It seemed
that every rogue had set up camp:
dandelion, sow thistle, white nettle, dock,
the path disappearing under scutch grass,
brambles and bindweed running amok,
but we cleared the ground, for lawns
to wind around dahlia, delphinium, damson,
and our favourite, the blue-belled jacaranda,
pebble rivers running through green seas
to quiet corners, the honeysuckle arbour,
we'd sit for hours, free of others,
and while away summer.

Our haven taken, smashed to smithereens.
Now there is only me –
from strange windows I watch foam ride the sea.
Soon, I'll shuffle to another room. In the darkness
the same stars still come through for me.

A FISH OUT OF WATER

At the creation of your species
you were given the habitat
you needed – a sea to live in.

The sea swelled and spread,
as if impressed
with its own abilities, drowning

mountains, the full-grown,
the bud, the just sown –
trees, animals, people,

altering the terrain of the earth
to a mass of ocean
without a feature.

You were brought in
to different dark, confined
to quarters – a fish out of water

in an ark full of oddness, that was
bellowing, barking, roaring, hissing,
squawking, whispering, talking,

the stench, the fangs, the claws,
the babble of languages
you know nothing of.

If stepped on once
by the ponderous elephant
you'd be squashed to pulp.

Our questions endless,
the how, of everything about
this bizarre business, gets to us.

Nevertheless,
you emerge fit for purpose –
to go and replenish the earth.

REPOSSESSED

Did you think
when you left me
to the salt-sprayed winds
and the traffic,
to the whims of vandals,
till my wrought-iron gate
black-blistered,
till thistles and grass
choked my concrete paths,
my doors and windows
rusted in,
I had nothing more to give?

Where prayers once rose
like incense
the swallow
is sitting on her eggs,
the wren
feeding her babies
in a rejected
mud cup nest,
the pipistrelle family,
clicking chirping
bundles of black-eyed fur,
packed into the cavities,
the Araneida spiders
filling the corners
with delicate embroidery.

THE CIGARETTE MAN

Miguel, black-haired,
moustache greying,
swarthy, muscular,
picking up daily,
cigarette butts, one by one,
from shingle, brick paving,
earthen paths, stone flags,
pristine sand.

With his haul
of cigarette trash
he builds a white-bearded man
in a tortoise-shaped hat,
and trainers,
adds a black dickie-bow,
a name in bold
running from chest to waist – NICO;
final touches – smoking a reefer,
wearing a medallion
saying: Nicotine Assassin.

Miguel dresses smart,
black trousers, white shoes, and shirt,
picks his spot, the busy part –
discotheques, souvenir shops, bars.
Nico and a bundle of butts beside him
the message is stark.

He continues
picking up, freeing
his beloved island
of toxins, plastic fibres,
that would poison the sealions,
the grey marine iguanas,
their land brothers,
in slack yellow jackets
and yellow pebbled faces,
the snow white,
blue-footed boobies
with their long orange beaks
curved at the end like tongs,
saltbrush sprawl,
sesuvium strewn with pink stars,
morning glory trumpeting
purple flowers.

RELEASE

White as the arctic,
waiting
on the quarry floor
in Carrara,
for something important:

taken to the city of Botticelli,
Angelico, Donatello,
to be transformed
into something imposing
enough, to stand
on the heights with Moses,

but you were weak,
too many perforations,
abandoned
to the elements
for decades.

An artist more forgiving
of your rough exterior,
an affinity with the language
of your veins, saw into
the dark of you, and, in time
would bring to light
something sublime.

He rarely left your side –
sleeping only in snippets.

Hammered, chipped,
chiselled through wind, rain,
sun, the spit and swirl
of marble dust until

he had freed
the mop of curls,
the eyes, engaged,
the turn of the torso,
the muscular limbs,
the stone in the hand,
a little of the sling.

THANKS TO ODETTE

Bob lives in a land of orchids, beaches, forests, cossetted by the
sun.
On cerise web feet, fine-gauge needle legs, button-ankles,
brandishing a bevy of salmon-coloured fluffed up feathers.
Traipsing the tiles, preening, eyeing himself in the vending ma-
chine.
He can be seen behind the wheel, or swimming in the cerulean
sea,
exhibiting his skills – raising his pink neck, bringing it down to an
S,
fanning out his huge wings, like something you'd see in Bur-
lesque.
Looking dapper – with his black boomerang beak, and white
flashes.
An attractive ambassador, his beauty enough, to speak up for his
own kind.
Much love, care, given to bring him this far, from lying on the
path
injured, from a crash into the window of the Hilton, to the Carib-
bean star.
Not strong enough to survive the rigours of the wild, neverthe-
less,
getting respect, interacting with children in a Curacao classroom,
on a mission, to prevent birds dying from plastic, metal, lines left
from fishing.

THE IRISH AND THE ENGLISH

The Celtic blood runs through her veins
and when the English came
then Ireland proved a harder land
than other lands to tame.

A rebel heart was ever hers,
her sons would always fight.
If money were not half so scarce
they'd drink the drink all night.

Her scenery is the stuff as could
intoxicate a man:
it holds as true if in Tralee
or by the river Bann.

And Erin's beauty is retold
A thousand times and more
by those who've left her sodden earth
to seek another shore.

They'll live upon the legends,
Saint Patrick he'll be theirs,
to force the Brits from Ireland
will be their fervent prayers.

They'll wear the shamrock once a year
and drink the whiskey dry,
they'll craic the crack of this 'n' that
and mist the wistful eye.

But Irishness is fleeting fast
as other things entice:
where men are moving up the scale
nostalgia will suffice:

they're English now the ties that bind.
What irony it seems
that Irishmen of all men
in England chase their dreams.

POCAHONTAS

How the great Powhatan loved her,
loved his little Pocahontas,
loved his sprightly little daughter,
for she sparkled like the jasper
used to make the finest arrows,
brought him gifts of bubbly laughter,
brought him sunshine with her chatter;
running softly, soft as snowfall
with the words Powhatan told her,
with the wisdom from her father
for the Paleface by the river,
loved to be among the Paleface
watching, laughing at their strangeness.
But her brother spoke with hatred:
"Paleface take, and go on taking".
Little Princess Pocahontas
watching fearful, watching closely
when her brothers brought a Paleface
back to Werowocomoco.
Though the great chief made him welcome
yet her brothers set upon him,
pulled their knives out of their covering.
Like the deer that runs from danger
Pocahontas ran to Paleface:
in her arms his head she cradled
like a mother tends her baby,
with her tears she kept on pleading,
with her pleas she won his freedom.
Great, the matters of peacemaking

yet, a little child did lead them –
little Princess Pocahontas
helped the Paleface love the Indian.

STRATHNAVER

While the champagne corks are popping,
glasses rising high
and everyone is toasting
the Scottish and English tie

there is always, always someone
whose heart is in despair
from things too terrible to tell,
from things that happened there:

where the highlands held their children
upon a windswept breast
as their tears ran down the dry-stone walls
and fear gave them no rest;

as their anguished cries were carried
on the wind, till they were spent,
and the hills became their open grave,
the wind their death lament,

for what was done by Englishmen,
and those in English pay,
left Highland children wounded deep.
Time will heal they say.

Through the decades and the centuries,
in the mountain and the glen
Highland children go on hurting
till their land is theirs again.

When the anniversary bells
are ringing in the square,
and the two-pound coin is proudly struck
to mark the happy pair

there is always, always someone
whose heart is in despair
over what was done in Strathnaver –
the tears in the heart, are still there.

HEALING IN THE RAIN

They walk the same earth
in circles that do not touch,
an earth cracked from thirst,
milk yields are down:

Willem rides his chestnut mare
more often around
his sprawling acres,
checking on his dairy herd,
testing the ground.

If only the rains would come.

He thinks of Adem, his son,
in demographics, building
a better South Africa
and his furrowed brow relaxes.

Gadusa tries to break up
the red clods of the Bantustan
with spade and fork, plants
cabbages, keeps a few chickens.

If only the rains would come.

He worries about the taxes
for the Chieftain,
about S'bu his son –
there is no work for the young.

Commotion in the city filters
down to the village, till the air
bristles with snippets
about gold in Witwatersrand,

the young men and women
abandon their homeland
to the old, and children,
the village withers.

Manor houses,
walls, fences,
rise in Johannesburg,
ramshackle huts
cling to its edges.

Out of the young
anger, retribution boils
and spits until
someone takes a gun
to settle it –

Adem is dead,
slumped in his office chair,
his pen dripping blood.

S'bu, caught
like a ram in a thicket,
eyes empty,
no remorse, no resistance –
to be hanged at midnight.

Gadusa crumples
to the ground sobbing,

for his son beyond saving,
for his own failure,
for the innocent life taken.

He goes to Willem
with nothing to offer,
but tears of sorrow.

They climb the hill together
slow, stilted, unable
to shed the heaviness
of things too broken
to be made whole.

Each alone in his own dark.

In that dread hour
the sky starting to change,
the wind playing
in the leaves of the baobab tree,
a drop of rain . . .

EGOLI

No connections, a few farmers
trying to make a living out of land
not even a tree can stand on.

Someone sees a gleam
in the eye of Witwatersrand,
the potential for rich pickings –

a gold vein in your foundations
brings you status, triggers
an avalanche of dreams

for which you'll be hammered, clawed,
beaten. Multitudes on the move:
Mozambican, Zambian, Angolan,

German, British, American, uprooting
to cross an ocean, trek the long stretches
of desert and veld, to get to you:

prospectors, labourers, hawkers,
miners from Kimberley and Cornwall,
engineers, bankers, lawyers;

acres of flat open spaces filling up
with food stores, liquor clubs, music halls,
boarding-houses, roads, railways;

mansion and ramshackle, euphoria and anger,
congestion and separateness; brutality -
a city that rivals Pretoria?

The tribe is broken, ideals do not hold.
They call you Egoli – City of Gold.

HOPE COMES CRIMSON

In endless dark,
under grass, a tiny seed
lies inert while worms,
in silent industry
affirming life, pass,
but you need light.

Out of the shell's craters,
out of the graves and trenches dug,
out of the wagon's lumbering,
out of the churning mud,
out of the knee's buckling,
the slippage, the stumbling,
out of the blood you come,

red petals fluttering like a butterfly,
and as delicate a touch,
bearing seeds a hundredfold
among the blackened stumps.

LOCHNAGAR CRATER

Staring into a vast bowl
it felt like half the globe had gone,
that I was standing on the edge
of the other half seeing something raw:

grass stunted, sparse, clinging to walls
of chalk, deeper than eyes can reach
the dead of both sides
sharing the Somme soil –

their name unwritten.
A short distance a simple wooden cross
on a white plinth keeps vigil
receiving tributes:
a cross, a wreath, a loving thought,
remember –
go gently, keep the peace. . .

THE KNOCK AT THE DOOR

The mountains home in summer
I had been running
into curtains of clear water,
chasing my brothers across
the spongy floor of the forest,
dancing in a field of clover –
pirouette, écarté, arabesque,
I *was* Anna Pavlova.

After having bagels, blintzes, apples,
I picked mushrooms and berries,
pushed them into my pockets
and ran home, ahead of my brothers,
to give them to mother,
she beamed at my thinking of her.

That evening, sitting on the floor
of our cottage leaning on daddy's knee,
listening to Mielec and Rubin
bringing music from the strings
of violin and cello, everyone
singing the songs of Purim.

A knock at the door, a thump,
mother opened and a jackbooted
soldier, almost pushing her over,
stomped in, ripped out the radio,
the telephone, commanded
we sew yellow stars onto our clothes . . .

SCRAPS

The trains keep coming,
disgorging hundreds
of people to a place
where the fences are double:

a guard, field grey
woollen coat and cap,
leather boots,
a loaded carabiner
slung over his shoulder,
watching from his high tower
well clear of the barbed wire,
inured against the stench,
devours a chunk of bread
down to its edge, tosses the crust
into the scrapyard of human remains.

A rush of children
from the wasted shadows
pounce like jackals,
fight over the crumbs.

THE BLANKET

It wasn't special in the sense
of a pure lambswool,
or brightly coloured,
patterned, or satin-edged;
it was dull, it was rough.

Those who came, to tell us
it was over, tried to wrench it
off my mother, she held it
tight, as if it were a diamond
of the first water.

It was our constant companion
on the long march of madness:

by day, driven like cattle
up the mountain tracks,
my mother, in her forties,
stooped, carrying
my little brother on her back

trying not to stumble,
or you'd get a rifle butt
jabbed into your back,
too slow, or fall,
you'd be shot, the dead
kicked over the edge.

My mother getting frailer,
kept on, putting one foot
in front of the other. I was filling up
with hate, done with God;
she never lost her faith.

At night she lay the blanket
on the mud, spread it out,
and out, gathered us in
on that small piece of comfort
to pull us close, and sing.

The soldiers edgy, cut-glass
efficiency slipped, fingers
more ready to pull the trigger.
I thought to myself, who will know
any of this, if none of us makes it.

Those who came that day,
to tell us it was over, didn't get it –
the mud-caked blanket was precious.

THE OTHER SIDE OF THE MOUNTAIN

A great wind whooshes into her,
rain dirties her dress with oily black stains.
She runs to the shaddock tree
and stands under – waits and waits
for her mummy to come back from Urakami

and tell her why the rain is all muddy,
why there's a monster eating the sun,
about the strange wind trying
to knock her down – she wouldn't mind
any of it if her mummy would come.

Fuje, Sadako, Urata, Mr Tagawa come.
They just keep crying and saying,
"Poor little Kayano" and she just keeps
watching, watching, for her mummy
to come back from Urakami.

Her daddy comes with the other doctors:
all bloody, and walks awkward,
as if his shoes are too heavy.
"Kayano," he says, "You don't have to run
and hide any longer."

She smiles a big smile,
for the shelter was damp and ugly,
but she wants her mummy back
from Urakami, it must be something
terrible that's keeping her from coming.

"Why are you so sad daddy,
why isn't mummy coming back,
why are so many people crying?"
she asks and asks. The doctors can't
stop people dying, there aren't enough coffins –

then the American soldiers come with chocolate.

HIBAKUSHA

A-bomb survivors

They had dug themselves
into holes. Staggered
out of them into ash and bone:

the doctor never tried
to save his wife
from being burned alive;

the daughter stayed
under cover rather than
go to find her mother;

the woman refused
one layer of her clothes
to a dying child who was cold.

In tents and shacks they try
to rebuild their homes.

It isn't long before
the blackened stumps are fruiting
camphor and willow buds;

street-cars clattering,
children at school again,
cafés serving sushi;

workers rebuilding
the prefectures, tangerines
in the market piled in pyramids;

the people worship in a new
cathedral; shadows remain,
the phantom voices do not fade.

NAGASAKI

A young woman
stands in the aftermath
disorientated –
everything in her world
has turned to rubble
in shades of black:

the cindered streets
are still hot;
charred bones lying
alongside melted roof tiles,
deformed sake bottles,
warped frying pans;

the stench
of incinerated flesh clings;
the only semblance
of another human being
an image, burned
into a concrete step;

she cannot cope
with something this grotesque
terrified there is nothing
to hope for left.
Her senses quicken –
in the air, Chrysanthemum.

Who knows

if the borders of the world
will be altered,
this place look the same tomorrow,

if these trees,
wintering between
deciduous and evergreen,

turned white
by some earth-shattering fear,
as if done with life,

but they still hold
through air that chills
their lifeless limbs,

as though waiting,
for a softer season,
to put flesh on the bone.

OTHERWISE

Reflecting on the Ghetto Heroes monument in Warsaw

You were meant
to be an obelisk
paying tribute
to a self-imposed god,
his empire 1,000 years strong
and every Jew gone.

What do we see?

A memorial
impossible to ignore,
a replica of Jerusalem's
sacred wall bearing
the last band of partisans.

For all the limitations
of inanimate things
this is full of vigour:
written in their eyes,
their whole being,
an indefatigable spirit.

Jews sculpted by Jew.

Hebrews living on
in granite and bronze,
giving their nation
in every age a reason
to stand tall.

NO TITLE

The world she walks
is mapped different:

her school a wooden hut
with no windows,
books non-existent,
or the tattered cast-offs
from white children.

Nevertheless, delighting
in her year two reader,
carrying it home holding
it close, but hidden
under brown paper.

Drawn to whoops and cries
she stands on the other side,
her nose tight against the wire,
eyes, laden with longing,
widen, and widen at children

flying high on swings,
shooting down slides,
spinning round and round
on painted horses, colours
whizzing into dizzy rainbows.

Her eyes drop down,
she picks up her parcel,

half-looking back starts to go,
stops, starts, walks slow
the road home, kicking the stones.

UNTER DEN LINDEN

The Linden trees are blooming in Berlin:
they're not that far and scenting miles of air.
I'd be there if I could, but I'm shut in.

I stare at damp dungeon walls, imagine
I am free as summer, and walking where
the Linden trees are blooming in Berlin;

I miss the outdoor cafes, the friendly din
of old men's chatter, the chance to share.
I'd be there if I could, but I'm shut in.

Music pounding, as if thinking were a sin,
I pace the dun linoleum like a bear.
The Linden trees are blooming in Berlin.

Like lilies they neither toil nor spin,
a beautiful fragility where you see them, prayer
is easy – here, a desperate struggle to begin.

The cold eyes of the Stasi, that two-faced grin
grinding me down daily to despair.
The Linden trees are blooming in Berlin.
I'd be there if I could, but I'm shut in.

THE WALLPECKER

Anger seethed
inside me for half a century
I didn't need the conditions:
the checkpoint,
the form-filling.

Oblivious to the watchtowers,
the prowling Alsatians,
the soldiers caught
up in their own chaos:
half-minded to shoot,
half-minded to not,

I took a sledgehammer,
thumped thumped
the adamantine blocks,
through drenchings
from fire hoses,
water cannons,
kept going
on adrenaline
and chocolate,
cheered on
by the human caterpillar
lengthening,
revelling on the top,
thumped thumped
until the mortar started to crack,
the concrete crumble,

clawed my own bit
out of the Wall
before the bulldozer's
thunder, and everything
steel brick stone barbed wire
tumbled.

Sometime later
tons of rubble landed
in the airport:
fragments
sold as famous.

A STEP TOO FAR

I stood with them,
white and black Americans,
wearing my placard
that insisted Black Lives Matter,
raised the clenched fist

in solidarity
with those who fought,
before us, for the same dream –
to not be judged
by the colour of one's skin.

We choked the afternoon with slogans:
Resistance Is Justified,
My Life Matters,
A Badge Is Not A Licence To Murder,
we chanted longer, we chanted louder,

went further,
crashed through fences,
tore down whatever offended,
shattered windows,
burned buildings.

Afterwards, in the light of reason,
I saw how malleable I was,
melding into a movement
with a different agenda –

I had harmed the cause.

THE METTLE OF THE MAN

Lt. Colonel Robert Blair Mayne

Bronze suits you:
the properties
of tin and copper
combine to make
for sturdiness –
something you fostered,
were renowned for,
flaunted.

Eagles are cast in it:
strong legs,
eyes that see further,
nerve that holds
in storms where others
would take cover;
riding the updraughts
with panache,
often the loner.

You wore the badge
of brilliance – sword and flame.
Like Red Cloud a great
warrior: first to blaze into danger,
fierce going in for the quarry,
the signal you gave was certain
and your braves followed.

Consummate soldier,
rebel and rogue,
who wore the mantle
of leadership boldly,
could find joy
in nurturing roses,
in wandering the world of poetry –
I wish I'd known you.
Bronze suits you.

KASHGAR

To see the breaking of a nation
come to the ancient city
and see the empty spaces, the rubble
of a culture that outlived dynasties:

mud brick houses, supporting each other,
poplar doors, bright blue, green,
adorned with brass leaves, veiled women
perched at tiny windows:

ovens, pits, fired up for naan bread,
skewered lamb, smoky whiffs of charcoal mixing,
drifting, with sand from the Tamalakan,
women stitching doppas, men beating copper;

bazaars oozing saffron, sesame, cinnamon,
stacks, falls, of sequined silk, lace, satin,
shimmering royal blue, orange, vermillion,
necklaces, bracelets, in gold, silver;

the hutongs resounding with dancing, singing,
sheep driven to market by old men
on donkeys, muezzins calling to prayer
from mosques on cobbled street corners –

pushed to extinction with the bulldozer's demolition.

BRINGING THEM HOME

Sorrow being laid
on the steps of the legislature –
hundreds of children's shoes:
moccasins, sandals, trainers;

dozens of little orange flags
being planted
in a nearby swathe of grass;

cosmopolitan Canada
flying the maple leaf at half-mast,

for the past is not a foreign country,
it is here in Kamloops,
Saskatchewan, British Columbia,
Canadian to the core, it is ugly –

uncovered remains
of a thousand children
in their unmarked graves,
Inuit, Métis, First Nations.

No place for them:
taken to be trained different,
force-fed English,
their own language an evil,
to be got rid of, pummelled
out of them with
a needle in their tongue,

no food, or shoved
into a cupboard;

sun dancing, medicine bags,
totem poles, potlach,
purged from their system.
Hidden, when hunger, disease,
whippings, killed them, given
a stone with a number, or nothing.

Names, stolen, restored
on a huge red scroll,
there should be more –
thousands of children
still out in the cold.

The government,
shocked by its own image,
asks for forgiveness –

A beginning, the uncovering continues . . .

BREAKING POINT

His tendency to complain
remained after he'd gone to work:
a shadow, hovering
as she tackled a mountain of ironing
and headed towards dusk.

From where she stood
she could see Benevenagh
drowning in mist
and felt,
her sense of self drowning with it.

She reached for the last shirt:
meticulously ironing
around buttons
the colour of pearl barley,
collar, pockets, pleats, placket, cuffs.
She wished she'd done his first –
he was fussy about his shirts.

She hurriedly put the ironing board back.
Left nothing to chance:
gave the mirror a quick look,
for reassurance:
her lipstick was fine,
she deleted the dark bits under her eyes,
downed a glass of wine,
then, scrutinised:
all those things that shouldn't be there

she removed
for the last time.

She felt him closing in,
just like the night,
heard the crunch of rubber on stones
and knew,
something, definitely, wouldn't be right.

A MAN LIKE THIS

He is a soap and water man:
his daily ritual using pure bristle
to whip up white on his cheeks and chin.
With silvered steel shaped like a T
he clears paths across his skin
like a man used to doing such things
until there is no more white.
From a little cream flask
he splashes Old Spice into his cupped hand –
the sound of slapping on cheeks
as if he is affirming, to anyone who will listen,
he is clean and ready to face the street.

He cannot take to tee-shirt and jeans,
is more at home in Harris Tweed,
cavalry twills with a well-pressed shirt
in white or cream, the tie, he'd have it in pure
Welsh wool if he could, muted, in shades of green.

He keeps his grey suit good, for Sundays,
(exceptions are made for weddings and funerals)
wears it to church with burgundy silk:
a matching handkerchief peeping from his top pocket,
and his tan shoes polished
to stop the rain coming through,
and because of the unwritten rule: whatever your mood
you look after your clothes and shoes.

But casualness is creeping over everything,
feeding on faith and behaviour,
the fabric of his world weakening
until it is in tatters. He is not defeated:
for a man like this the things that matter to him
still matter. Like a Monet in a room full of Picassos
his way of looking at things is still valid.

SHE WISHES IT WERE NOT SO

As she looks for her father
she is the only one
walking the long corridor
past walls of stainless steel

and stone – windowless, cold.
She comes to the farthest room
on the edge of the world
and wishes it were not so:

that her father did not have to lie
shut off, side by side with others
whose lives are slowly slipping
from time in beds that almost touch.

Her father's face is flushed, has a sheen,
his great head of white hair splayed
on the pillows that need plumped up
again, his soft brown eyes are open;

she focuses on them,
but that easy exchange is gone,
the words coming out of him
are coming out all wrong.

'Oh this can happen after a fall,
give it time', she is told.
She wanted to scoop him up and go,
but his umbilical cord is filtering

life support into him and she wonders
how long for: hours, days –
she does not know, and the doctors do not know,
and the nurses do not know.

How she wishes it were not so.

AUNT DOROTHY – 100TH BIRTHDAY

Oh, how stern the face
of Nature; earth shifts
and shakes, solid things
disintegrate, man still spurns
the Light you walk in

that keeps you bright
as Morning Glory,
your smile, a sun rising,
reflecting something
of the Divine story;

you weave the feeling
of welcome with
stitches of silk thread,
on linen or cotton,
feather, satin, stem,

for coffee-table tops,
cushions, stools,
chairs, tray-cloths,
fire-screens, pictures
to dress the walls;

honouring your Master
with tasks of service –
easing the hill
that others must climb,
drawing alongside

bearing gifts you made
for the lonely, the sick,
the frail: a boiled cake,
a walnut loaf,
a pot of marmalade;

helping us lighten up;
with a little chuckle
giving us your name
when you've taken
a tumble – 'Calamity Jane'.

Thank you
for dappling our days
with laughter, the countless
ways you lighten the load
for others, and the singing,

with a passion undimmed,
through every chapter
of your living, helping
us render a sweeter offering
to Him, and still singing ...

.

SIR PATRICK MOORE

He didn't come
with the formality of the tutored,
more like a diamond in the rough,
frothy enthusiasm for the cosmos,
that never left him from his youth,
loomed into our living room television,
and we were hooked.

Charmed by the look:
the errant eyebrows,
the red-stringed monocle
wedged under one of them,
the hair in snowy tufts,
the wide dark suit
folding itself on his huge body,
the dented collar on his white shirt,
the navy and burgundy striped tie,
slashed with white, that wandered,
but the one he liked.

Words rushing from his tongue,
like a river in flood.
Space became interesting to the young.
We followed him
into the dozens of books he'd written,
into searching the night sky,
for the where of things.

We lapped up his liquid patter,
as though it came from the Pierian spring.
He mapped the moon and made it matter.

MOTHER AND SON

Slower now, rounded shoulders,
thin mottled skin, yet here she is,
a promise never broken – neatly,
methodically, placing his shirts,
underwear, socks, in a leather suitcase;
pressing them down, locking them in.

Soon she'll have another knick-knack,
to put in her glass-fronted cabinet,
a tiny chalet clock from Switzerland:
delighting in its daintiness, cuckoo
and pendulum, she'll place it, just so,
beside the silver-plated spoon from Belgium.

Come evening he'll set up the screen,
take her to see the Bernese Oberland:
snow-laden mountains, cable-cars,
shuttered houses, belled cows, creamy brown,
meadows of Fairy Thimble, Edelweiss, Androsace,
quaint towns with gothic cathedrals, rooftop baths.

LOVE COUNTS

Insane,
yet so precise,
evil came
venting hate,
harnessing hell
for the destruction of life
in the name
of some distorted faith.
Vengeance in the right hand
tore the glittering crown from its head –

a billion dollars' worth of pride fell,
into a sea of dismembered dead:

clouds so poisoned
they extinguished the sun,
flames so fierce they blazed to heaven
raging heat:
carnage, grief,
indiscriminate slaughter
on American streets
stunned us into disbelief
it could happen here.

Feeling so fragile,
overcome with fear,
our wounds gaping, bloody, deep,
love found strength
for words that wouldn't keep.

Men of compassion came
again and again
daring the flames of infernal might
to salvage life – drag, heave, push through
the murderous heaps, mangled metal,
jagged glass, concrete slabs,
of writhing sliding volcanoes
exacting revenge on salvation,
till those who had saved so many
lay dead in the street.

Hell had stared us in the face that day,
taken our dreams, seared our soul,
but courage rose above the scourge of hate
to say, love counts.

NAILS

Nothing to distinguish us,
all gun-metal grey,
ubiquitous – wherever
there are joins to be made:
soles to uppers,
legs to tables,
doors to frames.

For every thousand uses
a thousand more;
out of the millions
three were chosen
to hold the bridge
across the chasm
from earth to Heaven.

Who could ask for more?

ACKNOWLEDGEMENTS

Spring Fever	First published in Eretz Songs of Poetry January 2021
Freedom	First published in The Curlew by Wildwood Press 2019
No More Sea	First published by Preeta Press July 2021
River Roe	First published in CAP anthology 2017/2018
Museum	First published in Bangor Literary Journal 2018
Empire Tana	First published by Preeta Press July 2021
Maytime in the Dales	First published by Park Publications summer 2011
Turf Fire	First published by Orbis winter 2012
Brief Endurance	First published in Honest Ulsterman June 2015
Rio	First published by Preeta Press December 2019

Repossessed	First published in The curlew by Wild Wood Press 2017
Release	First published by Preeta Press July 2021
Pocahontas	First published in Writing Magazine May 2008
Hibakusha	First published by Shabda Press 2017
No Title	First published in Eretz Songs of Poetry winter 2021
A Step too Far	First published in Sunbeam anthology August 2020
Breaking Point	First published in Pulsar by Ligden Press September 2008